Presented to: Date

From: Edith Nattermann

On the Occasion of: 10/27/85

Your Emmaus Walk

W9-AHV-970

The
Beauty of
Sharing

LLOYD JOHN OGILVIE

The Beauty of Sharing

HARVEST HOUSE PUBLISHERS
Eugene, Oregon 97402

The Beauty of Sharing

Copyright © 1981 by Harvest House Publishers
Eugene, Oregon 97402

Library of Congress Catalog Card Number 80-8880
ISBN 0-89081-246-2

Printed in the Unites States of America

Design: Koechel/Peterson Design
Minneapolis, Minnesota 55406

Given to
Me for You

**"The grace of God which was given
to me for you..."**

Ephesians 3:2, NKJV

*T*he secret of life is that all we have
and are is a gift of grace to be
shared. Everything that happens to
us, all that we learn, everything we go
through, each delight or difficulty, pre-
pares us to develop deep, sharing relationships. We have been called, chosen and
elected to receive grace, unmerited favor.
Christ has loved us to the uttermost. In
our experience, His forgiving love is sheer
grace. We have not earned it, nor have we
deserved it. Life in fellowship with Him
has given us wisdom and insight. The
challenge to love Him with our minds has
provided us with knowledge. Daily we
discover new truth about who He is and
what life was meant to be.

But grace is kept only if it is given away. Everything grace has given us is for others. What a lovely way to live! When we go through the valleys of trials or stand on the mountaintops of victory, we are being prepared to enter into the difficulties and victories of others. We go through all of this so that we will be able to say those empowering words of empathy, "I know what you are going through—I've been there!"

Life is the school of grace equipping us for a ministry of sharing, developing the confidence that we can say, "Thank You, Lord, for what has happened. I can't wait to see how You are going to use what You have taught me in sharing with someone who will need just what I've discovered!"

The Gift of Christlikeness

"To become Christlike is the only thing in the whole world worth caring for, the thing before which every ambition of man is folly and all lower achievements vain."

Henry Drummond

*T*he sublime example of the beauty of sharing is Jesus Christ. He came to reveal what God is like and what we were meant to be. As the Son of God, He reveals God's nature; as the Son of Man, He makes known the potential person each of us is called to become. But the new persons you and I are to be cannot be realized by our trying harder or striving for perfection. Paul gave us the secret when he said, "Christ in you, the hope of glory" (Colossians 1:27).

When Christ takes up residence in us, He makes us like Himself. It does no good to say to ourselves, "I should be less selfish, more generous, a sharing person. I must make an effort to do better in giving myself away." That usually results in continued failure and self-incrimination.

What the Lord wants is an invitation like this: "Dear Lord, I've tried to think of myself less and of others more; I've made repeated attempts to be a sharing person, really caring for others; but I've failed miserably. Come into my heart, Lord Jesus. Transform my self-concern. I ask You to share Your love through my words, actions and involvements. Take over, Lord. Give me a new heart, a new will to serve You by serving others. You are my only hope of glory." The inadvertent result will be the gift of Christlikeness.

A Lovely Thing

"Whatever your hand finds to do, do it with your might...."

Ecclesiastes 9:10, NKJV

"Every man feels instinctively that all the beautiful sentiments in the world weigh less than a simple lovely action."

James Russell Lowell

A man stood beside me at the open grave of his wife. He grasped my arm and said, "How I wish I had her back—there were so many lovely things I'd planned to do for her!" We all know the feeling of remorse over things unsaid and undone. We think of all the kind and gracious things we should do, but the days slip by in the busy rush of responsibilities. When we are too busy to enact the lovely thoughts, we are simply too busy.

God Himself is the author of the good feelings which need to be enacted. Action on the basis of those feelings is obedience to Him. He has entrusted sharing His love to us. When we resist putting our thoughts into action, we cripple our relationship to Him.

Start today by acting on your lovely thoughts. Start a new past. Today can be the first day of a new life! Here's a prayer with which to begin.

Lord, thank You for placing in my mind loving thoughts and feelings for the people in my life. You gently suggest lovely things we can do to enact what's in our hearts. Starting right now, I am going to do what You direct in the specific acts of sharing what You motivate in my heart. Don't let me forget, Lord. Give me the will to act!

Amen.

I Need You!

> **"Share your life, and find the finest joy man can know. Do not be stingy with your heart. Get out of yourself into the lives of others, and new life will flow into you—share and share alike."**
>
> Joseph Fort Newton

One of the greatest compliments a person can give is to say, "I need you!" The words melt our hearts and impel us to want to help. We all need to feel needed.

A crucial part of the ministry of sharing is to be able to admit our inadequacies and say to others, "I need you!" We can be sure that if we can't say that to others, they will probably never say it to us.

Actually, confession of our needs is an expression of healthy self-esteem. We value ourselves enough to believe that we are worthy of another's care. Those who cannot express their needs usually end up unable to help others with theirs. An honest expression of needs makes possible a healthy marriage or a creative friendship.

It is true that only God can meet our deepest needs. No human being can satisfy all of our needs. He or she was never meant to. We were created for fellowship with God. There will be a restlessness, an emptiness within us until we rest in Him and allow Him to fill the God-shaped vacuum. The closer we grow in Him, the more we realize how much more we need Him. Yet, in His wisdom and desire that His children share His love with one another, God has ordained that aspects of our needs for Him can only be fulfilled when we seek Him together. He reserves dimensions of His power to be given as we endeavor to meet each other's needs.

Sharing the Gift of Mutual Need

When we think of sharing, our minds immediately leap to something we have to give away—a material gift, money, help or advice. Yet one of the greatest experiences of sharing is letting people know that we too have known (or know right now) times of failure, inadequacy and need. When we feel that we must have it "all together" before we become a sharing person, we will miss great opportunities God sends our way. If we are willing to share what the Lord has taught (or is teaching) in life's tight places, we become channels of His grace to other hurting people. Others need to know that they are not alone, that we too face turbulent times.

Don't wait for solutions, carefully packaged reflections on past victories or neatly worded theories to dole out. Become willing to be involved as a fellow struggler. What you are going through is a gift in which you will discover a deeper relationship with the Lord. But it is also your gift to someone else who's going through the same kind of challenge or difficulty. A trouble shared is a trouble cut in half!

We all make mistakes, but the greatest mistake is to try to hide them. We all have frustrations, but there is no greater frustration than trying to pretend that we don't have any!

Out of the Dungeon of Self

"The love of our neighbor is the only door out of the dungeon of self."

George MacDonald

Self-concern is a prison indeed! The more we think about ourselves, our needs and our desires, the more incarcerated we become. The reason is that we were created to share. Happiness is in interdependence, not independence. When we contradict God's plan, we get moody, down on ourselves, others and life in general.

The door to the prison of our own making must be thrown open to the world filled with people who need us. A bad mood is dispelled when we get involved in listening to others and helping them to solve the problems they are facing. We can feel badly about our own situations until we are confronted with what others are enduring.

When we are in the dungeon of self-pity, we need a fresh flow of grace from God. But He usually does not come to us in our prison of self. He calls us to join Him in what He is doing. If we want God, we must go where He is—with people in need, those who suffer, the lonely, the frustrated.

Think of three people who need you. Call, write a letter, go see them. You need them more than they need you. They are the door out of your self-imposed prison. Two things will always occur: the joy you bring to them and the joy you receive from the Lord for them. You, most of all, will be blessed!

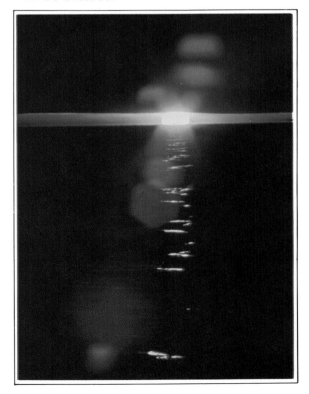

A Commitment to Share

"Commitment to Christ must involve commitment to our neighbor and our world, for Christ's sake."

Leighton Ford

"For this reason I also suffer these things; nevertheless I am not ashamed, for I know whom I have believed and am persuaded that He is able to keep what I have committed to Him until that Day."

II Timothy 1:12, NKJV

*C*ommitment is a crucial part of becoming a Christian and growing in Christ. We begin the Christian life with a response of faith to Christ's amazing love by giving as much as we know of ourselves to as much as we know of Him. Commitment is our part in realizing all that the Lord offers to us. It is an act of the will in which we yield total control of our lives and turn all of our relationships and responsibilities, the problems and the potentials, completely over to the Lord. The act of commitment opens the floodgates of the Lord's power in our lives.

There is no growth in this initial commitment without a commitment to share what Christ has done for us and given to us. When we commit our lives to share in Christ's name, He can use us in healing the hurts of others. Paul discovered that Christ is able! The words "He is able to keep what I have committed to Him" can also be rendered, "He is able to keep what He has committed to me." Both are correct translations of the Greek. The dynamic Christian life is being committed to what He's committed to us.

Have you ever made an unreserved commitment to be a sharing person? Exciting opportunities will happen when you do, and with each challenge Christ will be more than able to give you what you need!

We Are Christ's Gift to Each Other

When Jesus looked down from the cross, He saw not only the ignorant indifference of His executioners, but the anguish of His followers. The third word that He uttered from the cross was a request and a promise for which He was dying.

He saw His mother, Mary, and His cherished friend and follower, John. In a gesture of sublime love, He gave them to each other for mutual love and care. The sacrificial death He was dying was to break down the dividing walls between people so that the deep relationship of Christian fellowship could be possible. His mother and His friend were to be bound together in the divine bonds of love which would be the essence of the Church.

They were to care for each other as He had cared for each of them. Eventually they would find Him only in the deep relationship that their sacrificial love expressed for each other. He had to leave them so that they could go on to experience this further stage in the birth of the new creation in them and in the Church.

Note the differences in age, sex, personality traits, focus of interest. They were superseded by a new quality of relationship. The things which naturally divide people — even culture, education, background, interests — have little effect on Christian friendship.

Today Jesus gives the people in our lives to us. Once we release them to Him in a commitment to let go of our self-willed control, He gives them back to us to be cared for and nurtured in His love. Who're at the foot of the cross with you? They are a gift. If you want to know Christ, you will find Him by serving them in His name.

Knowing Where to Land

"Now we exhort you, brethren, warn those who are unruly, comfort the fainthearted, uphold the weak, be patient with all. See that no one renders evil for evil to anyone, but always pursue what is good both for yourselves and for all."

I Thessalonians 5:14-15, NKJV

People are like islands. Sometimes you have to row around them before you know where to land. Each person's needs are different. In the Christian fellowship, we are responsible for one another. When we listen attentively and care deeply, we are able to love profoundly. Paul reminds us that some need a warning, others comfort, some uplifting, and all require patience. Christ in us guides us in what to say and how to say it.

We are to talk to Him about people as much as we talk to people about their needs. He will give us an x-ray vision of the unique and special needs of each person. But we cannot give what we do not have, nor can we communicate what we are not receiving. As we allow Christ to deal with us, we learn how to communicate with people. Paul describes gracious Christlikeness. That quality can be ours in our dealings with people today.

Think of the people in your life who fit into the various categories that Paul lists in these verses. We are given the awesome opportunity to lift burdens today. A pastor friend of mine made a call at a home where tragedy had struck. The little son of the family met him at the door, then ran to his mother exclaiming, "Mommy, our friend is here, and he has brought Jesus with him!" Ah, I would that that may be said of you and me today!

Pass It on!

*"It only takes a spark to get
  a fire going,
And soon all those around can
  warm up in its glowing.
That's how it is with God's love;
Once you've experienced it,
You spread His love to everyone;
You want to pass it on."*

Kurt Kaiser

**"You can give without loving, but you
cannot love without giving."**

Amy Carmichael

*T*here's an old saying, "You can't take it with you!" Not true. What is implied is that we can't take our possessions with us when we die. But we will take our soul—the inner person made up of mind, intellect and will. That indestructible portion of us which exists beyond death's door will be eternally affected by what we believe and what we have shared because of what we believe.

When Christ is the Lord of our lives, we will want to share Him, His love and the material resources we have received from Him. We grow as healthy, mature people as we share. Heaven is a glorious eternal life of sharing with God, the whole company of heaven. Helping the living on earth, we become angels with a ministry of intervention. Sharing what we are and have is the best preparation for heavenly life. We will take with us the person who has been prepared to enjoy what God has prepared.

We will be uncomfortable when we meet the sharing heart of God if we have refused to share here and now. If you died today, would you be ready?

The Linus Limit

**"I love humanity;
it's people I can't stand."**

Linus—Charles M. Schulz

*J*esus Christ came to save humanity,
but His love was always personal. He
had time for people. In a crowd, His
attention was always focused on the person in greatest need. He consistently lived
the love He preached.

I am leery of people who say more than
their lives bear out. Often those who
make the loudest noise about human
need and wring their hands over human
suffering are the least involved in caring
for individuals. We have no right to or-
ganize movements, start great causes and
lead others unless we are living out what
we say in specific circumstances and with
specific people. It is easier to love humanity in general than people in particular.

When Jesus was moving through a
crowd, a woman who had been ill for
years pressed through the crowd, seeking
to touch the hem of His garment. She
kept saying, "If I can only touch Him!"
When she did, He stopped immediately.
"Who touched Me?" He asked. The disci-
ples were astonished. How could the

Master ask that with thousands of people thronging around Him? Yet He was God particularized, caring and sharing incarnate.

The story tells us that He knows and cares whenever we seek to touch His healing power. Christ is the sharing heart of God not only for humanity, but for people, people like you and me! The litmus test to determine our level of personal commitment beyond the Linus limit is to honestly ask ourselves how actively involved we are in specific sharing of our lives with individuals.

The Liberating Power of Affirmation

*T*he one need we never outgrow is for affirmation. We all long to be assured that we are cherished, of value and loved just as we are. Most of us know about our failures and inadequacies. What we ache for is someone to say, "I believe in you!" Affirmation gives us courage to be the persons we were meant to be.

Who in your life needs your affirmation? What could you say or do that would communicate your belief in that individual? Make this an affirmation day. Make a list of people who need affirmation and what you will say or do. Then see or call these people. Don't wait until tomorrow!

Affirmation is expressed delight. What God said at Jesus' baptism, He says to each of us: "This is My beloved Son in whom I am well pleased." Put your own name in that statement. In Christ, God affirmed you and me. He came for us, lived for us, died for us and was raised for us so that we might know how much He loves us. When we realize His affirmation, we can become affirmers.

Barnabas means Son of Encouragement. What we need is an Order of St. Barnabas, a fellowship of people who build up rather than tear down, who infuse hope and not discouragement, who believe that people can change when affirmed. I want to be a charter member. What about you?

The Everest of Ethics

"Therefore, whatever you want men to do to you, you also do to them...."

Matthew 7:12, NKJV

"Here lie I, Martin Elginbrodde.
Hae mercy o' my soul, Lord God;
As I wad do, were I Lord God
An' Ye were Martin Elginbrodde."

*T*his epitaph quoted by George MacDonald in the book *David Elginbrodde* humorously gets us to the heart of the motive of sharing. The truth, however, is that God is gracious to us far beyond our deserts. He loves us in spite of what we've done or been.

The question is, Can we do the same for others? Jesus' golden rule, often called "the Everest of ethics," is possible only through what God has done to and for us beyond what we have been able to do in return. We can do for others the things that we wish they would do for us only when we are motivated by His amazing grace.

The secret is that we are to do for others what God has done for us, not just what we would like them to do for us. The more we receive from our Lord, the more we will want to do for others. When we get in touch with our own needs, we become aware of the needs which lurk beneath the highly polished surfaces of others. Everyone has the same longing for love and understanding.

The Gratitude Attitude

"No duty is more urgent than that of returning thanks."

Ambrose of Milan

"O Lord, that lends me life, lend me a heart replete with thankfulness!"

Duke of Suffolk—Shakespeare
King Henry the Sixth, Part II, Act I, Scene i

I can remember it as if it were yesterday. I sat spellbound, listening to the profound teaching of the great scholar, the late John Baillie, in a classroom at New College, University of Edinburgh. Dr. Baillie was talking about the attitude of gratitude as the motivation of Christian service.

What he said was seared into my memory. "Gratitude is not only the dominant note in Christian piety, but equally the dominant motive of Christian action in the world. Such gratitude is for the grace that has been shown us by God. A true Christian is a person who never for a moment forgets what God has done for him in Christ, and whose whole comportment and whole activity have their root in the sentiment of gratitude."

The words warmed my heart. I knew then that I must spend my life sharing gratefully what God had done for me. Whenever I get tired or momentarily discouraged by the slowness of progress in working with people, I reread those words. They have become a mandate to give myself away. Returning thanks to God is sharing with others.

Andrew Murray once said, "To be thankful for what I have, and for what my Lord has prepared, is the surest way to receive more." There is an even surer way: to give what we have been given.

Sharing the Future

"For I know the plans I have for you, says the Lord. They are plans for good and not for evil, to give you a future and a hope."

Jeremiah 29:11, TLB

People need us to believe in their futures. A sharing person is one who can infuse expectation about their tomorrows. When Christ lives in us, we believe in the future more than in the past. A Christ-filled person is one who knows that however great the past has been, it is pale in comparison to what God has planned for the future. Yesterday is past; tomorrow is wide open with possibilities!

The world needs people to share the excitement that Joshua communicated to the people of Israel when they were more concerned about what God had done than what He was about to do. "Consecrate yourselves, for tomorrow the Lord will do wonders among you" (Joshua 3:5, ASV).

One of the most creative ways of sharing hope for the future is to help people to picture their dreams. There are so few people with whom we can unashamedly throw caution to the wind and dream a bold dream. God has plans for us, and we need fellow visionaries to share the conviction that the best is still to be!

"There are better things ahead than any we leave behind."

C. S. Lewis

The Unfinished Task

"I now rejoice in my sufferings for you, and fill up in my flesh what is lacking in the afflictions of Christ, for the sake of His body, which is the church...."

Colossians 1:24, NKJV

The words leap from the page. What is lacking in the afflictions of Christ? Was His saving work on the cross incomplete? Was something left out? No, but the finished work of Calvary must be communicated to every person who does not know Christ. That will mean sharing the sufferings of Christ. When we really care about people, it causes heartache and sometimes heartbreak.

The salient thrust of this passage is that we must die to our own selfishness and become involved with people and their needs. It is a paradox: the finished work of Calvary is "lacking" until the love of Calvary is presented to every person. When we are willing to give ourselves away and love people unqualifiedly, we will know the reality of the cross. Who is on your agenda?

A powerful story is told of Leonardo da Vinci. One day in his studio he started to work on a large canvas. He labored over it, carefully choosing the subject, arranging the perspective, sketching the outline, applying the colors and developing the background. Then, for some unknown reason, he stopped with the painting still unfinished. He called one of his students and asked him to finish the work. The student was flabbergasted. How could he finish a painting by one of the world's truly great masters? He protested his inadequacy and insufficiency for so challenging a task. But the great artist silenced him. "Will not what I have done inspire you to do your best?" he asked.

That is really Jesus' question, isn't it? He began it all 2,000 years ago. His life, message, death, resurrection and living presence started the great painting of the redemption of the world. He has given us the task to finish the painting. But there is a difference. Da Vinci left his student alone; Jesus never leaves us. He has given us the color palette and brush, and He whispers His guiding insight to us at each uncertain stroke. We cannot shrink from the task. The challenge and inspiration press us on.

Prayer Is Sharing

**"Pray for one another,
that you may be healed."**

James 5:16, NKJV

*P*rayer for others is profound sharing. It focuses our concerns about people in the heart of God. We share God's nature when we talk to Him about people, and one of the greatest gifts we can share with people is to pray for them.

Mother Teresa of Calcutta said, "Prayer enlarges the heart until it is capable of containing God's gift of Himself." We do not believe in the power of prayer, but in the power of the Lord who answers prayer. J. Edwin Hartill said, "Prayer is the slender nerve that moves the muscle of omnipotence. Prayer is simply intelligent, purposeful, devoted contact with God, or as Clement of Alexandria put it, "Prayer is conversation with God."

In that light, tell God what is on your heart today, as one unloads one's heart to a dear friend. People who hide no secrets from each other never want for subjects of conversation; they do not weigh their words, for there is nothing to hold back. Neither do they seek for something to say; they talk out of the abundance of their hearts just what they think. That is the way we are to talk and listen to God.

Prayer is the mother tongue of the people of God. Archbishop Trench exclaimed, "Prayer is not overcoming God's reluctance; it is laying hold of His highest willingness." Listen to the Lord in prayer. Get His perspective on your concerns and problems, loved ones and those people you need to learn to love. Spread it all out before Him. Say with Samuel, "Speak, Lord, Your servant listens."

Christ Makes up the Deficit

"O to grace how great a debtor
 Daily I'm constrained to be!
Let Thy goodness, like a fetter,
 Bind my wand'ring heart to Thee...."

Robert Robinson

"He who says he abides in Him ought himself also to walk as He walked."

I John 2:6, NKJV

The bottom line for a Christian is always red. Outgo must exceed income. When it comes to giving ourselves away to others in creative, healing, forgiving love, our relational books will never be balanced. Love is a careless spendthrift when it comes to the needs of people—regardless of what they do in return!

We are called to give more of ourselves to others than we either expect or demand to receive from them. If we take Jesus seriously and John's admonition sincerely, we will be in the red. "Anyone who says he is a Christian should live as Christ did" is The Living Bible translation. By living that way we can be assured that Christ will more than make up the deficit by His indwelling Spirit.

Stingy Receivers

"And whatever you ask in My name, that will I do, that the Father may be glorified in the Son. If you ask anything in My name, I will do it."

John 14:13-14, NKJV

We cannot share what we do not have! Therefore, the first step in discovering the beauty of sharing is to become an open receiver. The more that we allow God to give us, the more we will have to give away. We often talk about stingy givers. The reason they give grudgingly is that they have been stingy receivers. The root of the problem is our pride, self-sufficiency and arrogance. God wants to give us Himself, His gifts of intervention in our problems, His abundant mercy in our failures.

When Jesus visited the home of Simon the Pharisee, the banquet was interrupted by a woman who washed Jesus' feet with her tears of gratitude. The Pharisee was enraged. What Jesus said to him is for all stingy receivers in every age. He told him the parable of the two debtors. One owed five hundred denarii, and the other fifty. (A denarii was worth about twenty cents.) The creditor forgave them both.

"Tell me," Jesus asked, "which of them will love him more?" Simon responded with the obvious, "I suppose the one whom he forgave more."

Then Jesus drove the point home. When He had entered Simon's house no one had washed His feet, a kiss of peace had not been given to Him, and no one had anointed His head. All of these were customs of hospitality and blessings. But the woman, out of gratitude for the forgiveness Christ had previously offered her, had invaded the propriety of the banquet because she had to express her love. "Therefore," the Master said, "I say to you, her sins which are many are forgiven, for she loved much. But to whom little is forgiven, the same loves little."

Simon's pride needed forgiveness as much as the woman's sins. If he had received the love Christ freely offered, he would have been able to share his gratitude with Christ and others.

Sharing Without Strain

"You have not chosen Me, but I have chosen you and appointed you that you should go and bear much fruit, and that your fruit should remain, that whatever you ask the Father in My name He may give you."

John 15:16, NKJV

*H*udson Taylor, the great missionary hero and founder of the China Inland Mission, found the secret of sharing without strain. At one point in his life he was discouraged and depleted. He struggled to get more of Christ in his life. He prayed, agonized, fasted, made resolutions, read the Bible; but the serenity, vitality and power he sought eluded him.

One day he received a letter from a caring friend. The last paragraph was an arrow of truth from God for Taylor. "Not striving to have faith," it read, "or to increase our faith, but looking to the Faithful One seems to be all we need. An abiding in the loved One entirely, from time and eternity." Hudson Taylor was amazed at his own blindness. "I'll strive no more," he said. "It was all a mistake to try to get the fullness out of Christ. He has promised to abide in me. I am part of Him. Each one of us is a limb of His body, a branch of His vine."

After that day people noticed a change in Hudson Taylor. He labored, prayed, disciplined himself harder than ever, but not with a sense of strain and agony. He now radiated a magnetism of love and joy, for he was no longer a man who struggled, but a man who was being used. The Lord wants the same for all of us.

Hilarious Sharing

"Let everyone give as his heart tells him, neither grudgingly nor under compulsion, for God loves the man who gives cheerfully. After all, God can give you everything that you need, so that you may always have sufficient both for yourselves and for giving away to other people."

II Corinthians 9:7-8, Phillips

*T*he Greek word for cheerful is *hilaos* from which our word "hilarious" comes. Paul calls us to be hilariously free in giving what we have been given. That level of freedom comes about when we know that we have tapped into un-limited resources. God supplies all our needs so that we can become involved in sharing joyously.

There is a giving barrier which must be broken through as an aircraft breaks the sound barrier and then is free to soar. That barrier of "What's mine is mine" is broken only when we are overcome by God's love, His willingness to give us more than we need, and the fact that He has a strategy to meet people's needs through us. A truly joyous person has discovered that life and its resources are lent to be spent. If we want to share the heart of God, we must join Him in what He's been doing since creation—sharing!

"God has given us two hands—
one for receiving and the other for giving."
Billy Graham

Sharing Our Hope

"What oxygen is to the lungs,
hope is to the soul."

Emil Brunner

"Blessed be the God and Father of our
Lord Jesus Christ, who according to
His abundant mercy has begotten us
again to a living hope by the resurrection of Jesus Christ from the dead...."

I Peter 1:3, NKJV

"Always be ready to give a defense to
everyone who asks you a reason for
the hope that is in you...."

I Peter 3:15, NKJV

"Hope is nothing more than the
expectation of those things which by
faith we believed to have been truly
promised by God."

Moltmann

When Deborah Kerr was filming Quo
Vadis, she was asked by a newspaper
reporter if she ever feared the lions.
"No," she replied, "I have read the script!"
And so have we! We have been called to
be contagious communicators of hope.
Our hope is built on Jesus Christ, His
cross and resurrection. We know that we
are loved, forgiven and destined for
heaven. Therefore we can live with the
ambiguities and frustrations of life,

knowing that "all things work together for good to those who love God, to those who are called according to His purpose."

We have trusted our lives to a Lord who can bring good out of evil, can use all things for His glory and our growth, and who cannot be defeated by anything or anyone. Just as God could take the worst that man did at Calvary and give the best, the resurrection gives us hope not only at death but now. There's a saying, "Where there's life, there's hope." Not true! Where there's hope, there's life!

Do you have a vibrant hope? Is your hope based on a source which is ultimately reliable? Has that made you a hopeful person who can infuse hope in others? People need to see what hope can do for a person. Then, when they ask why we are hopeful, we can share the real reason for our hope. Matthew Henry was right: "The ground of our hope is Christ in the world, but the evidence of our hope is Christ in the heart."

How Can
I Help?

I have a friend who answers his phone by saying his name and then offering, "How can I help? Is there anything I can do for you?" The amazing thing is that he really means it! He is an open, giving, spontaneous man for others. To become a sharing person, communicate by word, attitude and facial expression a practical helpfulness. People can read the signals. Our body language speaks loudly: either "Don't bother me!" or "How can I help?"

Helpful Christians are people who have expressed the love of God who is a "help to the helpless." That's true of my friend. He's been through a lot of suffering and pain. Rather than hardening him to life, it has made him sensitive to the difficult battles others are facing. Anyone who has cried out, "God, help me!" and has received comfort and courage is then prepared to live a life of helping others.

*"God is our refuge and strength,
a very present help in trouble."*

Psalm 46:1, KJV

Sharing Life's Grief

**"Blessed are those who mourn,
For they shall be comforted."**

Matthew 5:4, NKJV

G rief is a many-sided sadness. It is caused by loss—the death of a loved one, a diminished or shattered hope, a broken relationship, an anguishing disappointment. In such times we need a friend who can share the heartaches. We need someone who will allow us to feel through our grief without giving glib, easy jargon.

Grief is like pus in a sore; it needs a poultice to draw out the pain. Our task is to be that to others when life falls apart for them. We are called to comfort by listening with love before we speak gentle words of encouragement. People need to know it's all right to express their grief, to get it out, and then to hear assurance that the Lord is there with them and He will not forsake or forget them.

After we've ached through the grief, there is a right time to help the person talk to God about the hurt in prayer. He will give us the right words, perfectly timed, for a communication of His comfort. The most important thing is to help the person surrender the grief to Him, the

Healer of the hurts of life. Any grief we
have gone through ourselves and given
over to the Lord's healing is in preparation for comforting others.

*"Blessed be the God and Father of our
Lord Jesus Christ, the Father of mercies
and God of all comfort, who comforts us
in all our tribulation, that we may be able
to comfort those who are in any trouble,
by the comfort with which we ourselves are
comforted by God."*

II Corinthians 1:3-4, NKJV

Sharing the Impossibility of Impossibilities

"For with God nothing will be impossible."

Luke 1:37, NKJV

"I thank God there is a way out through Jesus Christ our Lord."

Romans 7:25, Phillips

There is a famous painting in which the artist depicts the great encounter between Faust and Satan. Faust gambled for his soul. The painting pictures the two sitting at a chessboard, the devil leering because he has checkmated Faust's king and knight.

One day a famous master of chess went to the gallery in London to study the picture. He spent hours meditating on the seemingly impossible situation it depicted. He paced back and forth. Then, to the utter amazement of the other art viewers in the gallery, he shouted his discovery. "It's a lie!" he blurted. "It's a lie! The king and the knight have another move!"

There's always another move for God. However black and grim things seem, He has a next move we could never have imagined. Whenever we are tempted to say, "I'm done in, I'm beaten, there's no hope left," the Lord is ready for His big move.

Once we've experienced God's way out when we've found ourselves in a cul-de-sac of impossibility, we become people who can go to people who are worried and boxed in and say, "Be sure of this: God always has one more move!"

Effective Sharing of the Source

"I thank my God, making mention of you always in my prayers, hearing of your love and faith which you have toward the Lord Jesus and toward all the saints, that the sharing of your faith may become effective by the acknowledgement of every good thing which is in you in Christ Jesus."

Philemon 4-6, NKJV

We hear a lot of talk about sharing our faith. For many of us that means explaining theology or outlining the plan of salvation. Paul's affirmation of Philemon's effective sharing of the faith by communicating what Christ had done for him is the key for us today.

The world around us is asking, "Does this thing work? Can faith in Christ make a difference? Tell me from your own life what believing in Christ means!"

One of the most effective ways to share our faith is to acknowledge the source of all that we've been able to accomplish. We could not breathe a breath, think a thought, do our work, enjoy our talents, and attempt and do great things if it were not for the Lord's constant and consistent blessing.

When we are quick to point away from ourselves to our Lord, people will want to know Him and the same quality of life we've found in Him. Then we'll have the opportunity to introduce them to Him. Our first challenge is to live a life that demands explanation, and the second challenge will be to find time for all the people who will want to find the joy we have found.

"If you want favor with both God and man, and a reputation for good judgment and common sense, then trust the Lord completely; don't ever trust yourself. In everything you do, put God first, and he will direct you and crown your efforts with success."

Proverbs 3:4-6, TLB

A Tap on the Shoulder

"There is no surprise more wonderful than the surprise of being loved; it is God's finger on man's shoulder."

Charles Morgan

When we are motivated by an inner urge to share ourselves and what we have with others, we can be God's tap on a person's shoulder.

The other day I felt compelled to go see a friend. "How did you know I needed you?" he asked. "I had prayed for guidance in a problem I'm facing and really needed a friend to talk to. I guess I need to talk until I know what I want to say. God told me He would send someone, and here you are!" Imagine the joy I felt. What if I had neglected the nudging?

It is awesome to realize that God can use us as His messengers, healers and helpers. He's up to exciting things, and all He needs is a willing, receptive and obedient spirit.

"So, affectionately longing for you, we were well-pleased to impart to you not only the gospel of God, but also our own lives, because you have become dear to us."

I Thessalonians 2:8, NKJV

Fuel for the Flame of God

*A*my Carmichael's poem "Make Me Thy Fuel" is a daring daily prayer for our life of sharing. When we truly believe that the joy of life is sharing, this prayer of commitment is the charter for our caring.

"From prayer that asks that I may be
Sheltered from winds that beat on Thee,
From fearing when I should aspire,
From faltering when I should climb higher,
From silken self, O Captain, free
Thy soldier who would follow Thee.

From subtle love of softening things,
From easy choices, weakenings,
Not thus are spirits fortified,
Not this way went the Crucified,
From all that dims Thy Calvary,
O Lamb of God, deliver me.

Give me the love that leads the way,
The faith that nothing can dismay,
The hope no disappointments tire,
The passion that will burn like fire,
Let me not sink to be a clod:
*Make me Thy fuel, Flame of God."**

---

*Amy Carmichael, "Make Me Thy Fuel," *Toward Jerusalem* (1936; rpt. London: Society For Promoting Christian Knowledge, 1950), p. 94.

Photo Credits:
Dale Beers; page 55
Doug Coleman; page 53
Paul Eaves; pages 19, 33, 41, 43
Renee Lee Varia; page 31
All other photos by
Koechel/Peterson Design